Really Happy

Also by Jim Reese

ghost on 3rd NYQ Books, 2010
These Trespasses, The Backwaters Press, 2005, 2006

Chapbooks:

The Jive, Morpo Press, 2004
Wedding Cake and Funeral Ham, Grizzly Press, 2002

Really Happy

by

Jim Reese

The New York Quarterly Foundation, Inc.
New York, New York

NYQ Books™ is an imprint of The New York Quarterly Foundation, Inc.

The New York Quarterly Foundation, Inc.
P. O. Box 2015
Old Chelsea Station
New York, NY 10113

www.nyq.org

First Edition

Layout and Design by Joseph Hamersly and Raymond Hammond

Cover Art: "Really Happy," oil on board, 13 x 15 in., 2013 by Bret Gottschall | www.gotty.com

Author Photo by Jamie Ridgway

Library of Congress Control Number: 2014945817

ISBN: 978-1-935520-81-8

For Willow, Paige and Linda

and for Pauline Reese,
who always reminds me to laugh loud.

Acknowledgements

Grateful acknowledgements to the editors of the following journals in which these poems, sometimes in early versions, first appeared or are forthcoming:

"The Hard Nutcracker," "Snails Suck," "Feels So Good to Be So Fat," "April's Proposal," and "Unlimited Absolutes" *Clover—A Literary Rag*; "Buckfever" *Phoenix in the Jacuzzi Journal*; "As Hot as a Two Dollar Hooker at a Clown's Convention" *P3 Poetry and Art Exhibition* Washington Pavilion Sioux Falls, SD 2012-2013; "The Doctor vs. the Pre-Med Student" *Survive and Thrive: Starts with the Heart*; "Black Words on White Paper" *Paterson Literary Review* (Third Prize 2012 Allen Ginsberg Poetry Award); "Scratch and Win," "Knipplemeyer and Sons, We Lay the Best in Town," "German Dressing and Black Velvet," "The Blues in Jeans," and "The Saw Grinder" *Paterson Literary Review*; "Medley" PoetryMagazine.com; "The Fruit House" as "Hank's Fruit House," "As Hot as a Two Dollar Hooker at a Shriner's Convention," and "Breast Man" *New York Quarterly*; "Will You Sell That Eyesore?" *The Midwest Quarterly*; "Saluting Lieutenant Jones," "Sunshine, Handcuffs, Plexiglas, Scars," "Wishing Well" as "Free Willy," "Cattle Drive," "Jockeying for a Mate," and "The Relaxer" *Louisiana Literature: A Review of Literature and the Humanities*; "Ordering Take-Out at Broadway Lanes" and "Gothic Chic" *Lips*; "Pretty as a Grit" as "As Pretty as a Smoke" *Connecticut River Review*; "English 103: No Shoes Required" *Platte Valley Review;* "Man's Four Biggest Fears," "Fifty Shades of Grey," and "Potatoes are in the Dryer." *Harpur Palate;* "Really Happy" *South Dakota Magazine.*

Thanks to Raymond Hammond and the fine staff at NYQ Books for believing in my work; to George Bilgere, Patrick Hicks, Mike Reese, Kevin Clark, Marielle Frigge, Chuck Bowden, Jim Daniels, Neil Harrison, Lauren Janssen and Dana DeWitt who have seen many of these poems in their early stages and offered inimitable criticism. Thanks to Maria Mazziotti Gillan and the distinguished Poetry Center in Paterson, New Jersey.

Contents

Really Happy

Ready—Action!

I'm standing in line
at the mega-pharmacy, waiting to buy drugs.
I know, I don't like this place,
but it's handy and cheap.
Standing in this slow line,
I can't keep my eyes off the prophylactic section. Two young guys
with bottles of 5-Hour Energy shrug shoulders, laugh,
turn to look at who might be staring at them, joke louder,
turn back to the KY and rows of Trojans and Lifestyles
while they fondle the Astroglide.
Don't be such a numb-nut,
one says to the other as they snicker
and turn their cart down the aisle.

Soon enough, they're back. Intent this time
on grabbing the right product.
Then off they go, burying their goods
in a large half-empty cart that in a couple of years
they will fill with formula, baby wipes, diapers, Aquaphor Healing Ointment,
disinfectant wipes, lead paint test kits, hand sanitizers, lots of sugar-free juice,
binkies, tearless shampoo, a Pack and Play, a bouncy seat, pregnancy tests,
colored condoms, acid reducers, Band-Aids, Ativan, peroxide, and tonic.
The cart will overflow.
That will only be the beginning.

Today, though, none of that stuff matters.
They race for the only male check-out clerk who, God willing,
will let them pass through with hard-earned cash
without asking for their IDs, or if they need to speak
with the pharmacist about practical application,
correct procedures, or any other instruction
they've never wanted or been given.

Composition 103: No Shoes Required

The green shell of his backpack makes him lean
into wave after wave of responsibility.
—Ted Kooser

My students, most of whom
have never bought a book on their own,
lean eagerly on chairs towards the screen,
their eyes showing all their white.

They like DVDs more than books,
more than poems. One says, *I can relate.*
I'm so like totally more focused than when I read.
One student is shoeless.
Toes curled under—I imagine him hanging
upside down, sleeping in a tree.

A young woman in class
is wearing her Victoria Secret I LoVe PiNk
pajama bottoms and cougar-print slippers.
She looks cold, her hoodie pulled tight around her head.

The damn near scuffless cowboy boots in class are tied and the cowboy
has a holster for his iPhone.
Thumbs slowly evolving into fingers
as he texts his horseless way into the victorious sunset.
The only things missing are a pink dress shirt
tucked into jeans pulled up
too high, the belt buckle big and bronze.

There's a G-string arriving late,
bending now in front of the class
to pick up whatever it is she's dropped.
There's always a G-string. The batting of eyelashes.
What am I if I don't look? I preach immersion,
teach *show don't tell—*
write what you know well.

A student in the front of class keeps raising his hand.
I pause the video.
Are we supposed to be taking notes on this?

As Hot as a Two Dollar Hooker at a Clowns' Convention

At the head of the line, buying a twelver of Pabst,
a hairy, overweight man with a plumber-crack
and a t-shirt two sizes too small
drops a quarter on the ground.

He hesitates. He'll have to brace himself against the counter
and bend at the waist to pick up the coin.
He adjusts his pants—he hasn't yet seen who's behind him,
just a pair of pink sandals.

The cross-dresser in the sandals has on a V-neck blouse
and cut-off jeans. He's in his early twenties,
buying a six-pack of Smirnoff Raspberry Burst.
This is in South Dakota. Did I mention that?
Moccasins and flip-flops are still okay here, but pink sandals
have been banned in the state.

Time stands still as both men stare at the quarter.
Then the big guy braces himself and goes down—
one hand on the counter,
one hand going for the coin.

Excuse me ma'am, he says, as he comes erect.
Then their eyes meet, and he comes unglued.
Oh, for Christ's sake! he says.
I should have known.

Feels So Good to Be So Fat

I'm increasing my total strides
on the elliptical machine at the wellness and
fitness center, feeling adequate next to the large
man moving ever so slowly and uneasily
on the stationary bike next to me.
And I am in control
of the remote for once, watching
Man vs. Food.

Is this show really necessary? The large man barks.
Give me that remote.

I turn up the volume,
reassure him that it is necessary,
that if the host can consume
the Italian Challenge—seven pounds of chicken parmesan,
Italian sausage, lasagna, spaghetti and meatballs, manicotti,
a whole loaf of garlic bread, fresh salad, cannelloni,
a cup of Italian wedding soup, and an apple crisp dessert
in under 90 minutes,
he wins a t-shirt.

Only been done two times, I add, *ever.*

Increasing my resistance,
I watch my smart rate
heart rate
peak high.

Black Words on White Paper

I am grading freshman essays.
Too many papers about exhaustive
road trips without hitchhikers. Anorexia.
The death penalty. Abortions. One about the
Future Farmers of America. You don't have to
grow up in the country to be a member.
I never knew that.

Most essays about families say they are dysfunctional.
They always are.
But sometimes it still scares me what students reveal.
Like when Carlos writes, *That night,*
when my father pointed his hunting rifle
at my head and said he was going to put a bullet between my eyes,
I knew I had to say something. That's the first time I used my voice
to make a difference.

The phone rings and it's Willow.
Dad, she says, her voice shaky and exhilarated.
Can I get my ears pierced?
At that moment, she could have asked for a pony
and I'd have probably given it to her.

How exciting it is to hear a child's anticipation.
The delight, instead of
darkness.

The Fruit House

—for Neil Harrison

We don't fill out any job app,
just meet the dayshift boss who,
and I'm not kidding you, is straight-outta-movie-haggard—
inhaling his cancer stick and blowing smoke
right in Carlos' and my face, saying,
You're gonna be here tomorrow at seven in the morning?
Stepping all over his cigarette butt like that will teach it a lesson.
Don't be late, is all we hear when he turns the corner.

We aren't. We get here early and watch
one of the guys swallow his girlfriend's tongue
before he gets outta her car, everyone else dragging
their dead asses in for this twelve-hour shift.

Carlos is in the egg room.
At break in the pisser he's hacking out loogies
in the sink, saying he's never seen so many hard boiled eggs—has to
breathe through his mouth as he cuts each one in half
and hollows out the hard yolk.
Screw this place. I'm gonna quit. Making me sick.

Can't quit. I tell him. *It ain't even lunch yet.*
And I head back to the salad room where I continue to
rip the cores out of heads of lettuce.

Hit it like it's some fool's head, the supervisor says.

I continue to punch and rip
punch and rip
punch rip
until the heads form their own mountain of green in the corner.

Room supervisor is chain smoking and watering
the pile of lettuce with a garden hose.
Prewashed, he says and smiles,
spitting on the floor.

One by one the heads are thrown into this enormous grinder
while women gather at the other end,
bagging and tying
bagging and tying.

Here comes carrots from some other room,
boss man says chef salad, spits again
and alls I know is I'm boxing up these bags of salad and taping
them boxes shut until I can't get untangled and I'm all
a mess with brown packaging tape and boss man tells me, *Get out!*
And I do. Walk by the egg room, holler to Carlos,
Screw this place! Watch him smile
and throw his white gown and hairnet on the floor and we
are gone.

We know we have a few more years of freedom,
before we can never quit a job
again.

Man's Four Biggest Fears

Should be easy enough to answer. But, I'm only
one guy, with my own suspicions, concerns.
Who am I to say for sure?

I ask my father.
Google it, he tells me. And before I do he says,
Death, of course. Public speaking is probably another.
Scary – huh? He says, *Prison. That*
probably won't even make the top five.
I google the question.
Because that seems far easier
than doing the non-anonymous survey myself.

1: *Inadequacy.*
2: *Inadequate size of penis.*
3: *Freedom.*
4: *Being broke.*

It continues:
5. *Being perceived as gay.*
6. *Dying alone.*
7. *Ending up with the wrong person.*
8. *Keeping the spark alive.*

Inevitably the fears revolve back to masculinity.
This doesn't surprise me. That cliché prison phrase,
Three hots and a cot is even more believable
than before.

Jockeying for a Mate

The cover of the new Jockey catalog captures
a man and woman wearing pajamas in a wheat field.
I can't tell what county they're standing in,
much less what state. The clouds look familiar, but
it's barbed wire and round bales here.
To be honest, I can't remember the last sea of wheat
I've stood in.

The guy is squinting like he might be staring down a doe,
and the erect woman, she's not all that interested in him;
she actually looks like she's got her eye on some other buck.
He's got to be a little disappointed. I mean, really,
what kind of guy chases a woman all the way
out that far into the middle of a wheat field?

Stare too long at the picture,
and you see the guy has on a pair of jeans—
the wheat is almost up to his waist.
They're not fooling anyone. The woman is wearing a long-sleeved
onesie, which is odd. At the end of the day, really,
do we care more about the guy's legs or hers?

Think too long and you imagine the guy
is on a gluten-free diet, maybe he's allergic to wheat,
would die to be on the cover,
wants to save face.

The next day I get the skinny.
When I open the catalog, there they are
closer this time, at an old wooden kitchen table;
both have on new waffle thermals
and are spoon-feeding each other
Cream of Wheat.

Waitress in the Sky

Today, here at the Hilltop Diner,
I watch a man push in his chair
and the waitress come to clean up his mess.
The hostess rings up his ticket and asks,
You want to leave a tip, Doll?
The man looks over his shoulder towards the table.
The waitress' young daughter has come to help
play clean-up.

Here's a buck.

Well, thank you kindly,
sir.

The aura of waitresses
has always intrigued men. The working class,
firm asses of the women who
take orders and bring us food.
And let's not forget the allure
of the damsel in distress.

Of course
we're just customers paying
for a service. So the fantasy
of the highway diner's spicy mama
is just that.

But imagine a world of only waiters,
their greetings something like this:
Hey, Sugar. Would you like to try the morning delight?

Hear the shocked response:
Excuse me, young man, but what did you just say?

The waiter stone-cold and speechless,
slowly reaching to fill the coffee cup without
getting his hand slapped or scalded.

I would like whole wheat, lightly toasted,
and not burnt. You know the difference?
Two eggs, sunny-side up—cooked.
Bring me my steak black and blue.
And one last thing. I'd like some ice water.
Put two lemons in it, Doll—don't just drop them in.
Squeeze them like you mean it. You understand
what I'm telling you?

Yes. I believe I do.

Well then go on now.
Sugar.

Shirley Temple and a 7-10 Split

Shirley Temple is on her stomach spinning
on a stool at Ten Pin Lanes.
Her dad is bellied up to the bar
next to her. He orders a shot of Ten High
and a Budweiser back.
He drops the shot in and knocks
most of it back in one long swallow,
grabs the nearest bar rag to wipe off
what's left on his face, and orders Shirley Temple
another soda—with a cherry, of course.

She's only eight. I know this because
her parents drop her off at the pool;
she's there all day—her skin brown
and baked—that annoying kid who's always
pestering. I realize
I'm sorry for her and start to draw conclusions.

Thing is,
I spent many a night in bowling alleys
begging my dad's friends for quarters—
used to wet my fingers and touch metal screws
on two side-by-side pinball machines,
serving as a conductor, a live wire.

I stole change that men threw by empty beer pitchers
to play Asteroids.
I've stuck gum in the holes
of more bowling balls than I can count. That sweet smell
of oil on rag—the hand drying machine
while contemplating Mark Roth's
extremely unorthodox
attempt to pick up the 7-10 split.
Hell, who am I kidding? I grew up in alleys.
From Des Moines to Omaha to here in this town
with its six lanes, where the ball,
just like everything else,
still physically rolls back to you.

Snails Suck

Our goldfish have all gone
to the great aquarium in the sky.
To be honest, they don't last long here.
Swimmy hung around the longest
in a tank without a filter. *Dorothy Lynch*
came in a close second. *Lettuce,*
we found belly-up.
Stinky and *Brownie,* floaters at the top.
We found *Camouflage* half in, half out of the
filter. *Spots,* I can't remember, but
that fish died too.
So What's It To You,
I found this morning,
one of the snails sucking on its head.

Knipplemeyer and Sons, We Lay the Best in Town

Forgive me my transgressions and all the shit I've shared....
—Brent Best, *Slobberbone*

My best friend's dad, the block layer, said,
Hold this jackhammer up for a minute,
you skinny little pecker, and we'll let you come to the job site.

The same father we looked hours for,
who would turn to us as the sun shone into the entrance of the bar
wherever we were—Millard, North Omaha, Bellevue—
begging for money for smokes or beer, or
worst case scenario,
to tell him he had to go home.
You stupid dago wop bastard.
Get a job!
Get your fat ass outta here and take your hippie friend!

We wanted to be men, and we knew, even then,
this wasn't the way to make a home.
Searching Millard taverns for his beat-up rig,
stealing coins from his ashtray—we were
wrong then, too—saying we never found him,
never saw a thing.

All those manual labor jobs, busting ass to make a buck
so we could blow it on booze, breasts and skateboards,
where we'd tear up our bodies sess–sliding and launching off
ramps onto concrete, trying to impress girls,
winding up on our knees
praying to land our moves next time.

All that language that molded us,
all that language we wouldn't use around others,
all those words we took in and dished back only to each other.

When it was late, when we tried to dream
but couldn't shut out the voices—
couldn't turn off the noise of a garbage disposal grinding credit cards,
the *Go back to your room and go to bed!*
The sugar bowl against the wall.

We made amends.
We realized our families
were just as unstable as the rest.

And you know, we say the wrong things in families
of our own now. We scream too much,
love too much,
but don't let go.

Habit

I suppose it's just habit,
when I pass the guys in the yard—
How's it going?
Since I was a kid, I'd ask,
How's it going? To strangers—to friends.

Today, as I pass men in their prison-issued khakis
and numbered shirts, one stops and tells me,
Don't you know—you're not supposed to ask us that?
And those few seconds that we stand face to face—
I try to conjure up what I should say before a correctional officer
orders him away.

What I should have said was,
No, I didn't know. How stupid of me
not to think of something smarter to say.
Me, the teacher, who can leave this prison camp
any time I like.

The Saw Grinder

Grandpa, with your barrel chest punched out,
shirtless in your worn jeans and belt cinched tight,
I watch you climb
the oak tree in your front lawn,
toss you a worn-handled hacksaw with rusted teeth,
ask why pruning is necessary.

When you twist your limbs
among the tree's, lose yourself
and land flat on your back,
I hover over you screaming, *Grandpa!*
Grandpa! You dead?

Later, in the garage, I snoop through
Playboys my father gave you,
hear the toil and mince of ax on grinder,
saws sharpening, and *That god damn tree.*
I'll fix that son-of-a-bitch.

Thirty years later, I stand in your room
as two nurse's aides maneuver you into a wheelchair.
On your closet door, a sign:
My name is Cecil Brandenburg, my wife is Betty
and I am in Panama City.

Betty is gone now, Grandpa.
When I ask if you know why I'm here,
you smile and my mother shakes her head.
We wheel you across the parking lot to
eat ice cream. We talk some,
our old fishing tales
snapping in and out of consciousness.

I wheel you back to the home,
park you in front of a group of women,
place my hands on your bony shoulders—
The ladies are out today, Junior, the ladies
are out.

Yes they are, Grandpa.
Yes they are.

South Dakota Bumper Stickers—Redux

My Other 4x4 Has Legs

I love animals, They are delicious

The HICK LIFE

That's What She Said

I like my women like my deer: HORNY

I'd rather be hang gliding

I'm A Hot Tubber

BE THE FISH

I'd rather be riding her, too

I'd rather be CUMMIN than GOING

Save the Ta Tas

If it has tires or tits, it's trouble

I can muck 30 stalls before breakfast!
What can you do?

Absolute Car Credit

MORE COWBELL

Gayville Fire and Rescue

If the Fetus You Save is Gay,
Will You Still Fight for Its Rights?

Will Brake for Explosives!!!

Get the HELL Outta the WAY, Grannie's late for BINGO

Socialism Sucks

Native
Thunder Clan

Lock 'em and Drop 'em

Red Hair, Don't Care

Water Boarding is for Pussies

Green Bay **Fudge** Packers

If you don't like whiskey, huntin' and strippers, don't come here

Keep Honking, I'm Reloading

BEWARE THE MARE!

Save a Cow, Eat a Vegetarian

Eat More Kale

BACK OFF, City Boy

ALARM = Mastiff

IF YOU CAN'T STAND BEHIND OUR TROOPS, FEEL FREE TO STAND IN FRONT OF THEM

SAVE the Boobies

Cowboys for Christ

I MISS President Reagan

My other tractor is my neighbor's

It's not the destination, it's the journey

Silly boys, Jeeps are for girls

My kid defends freedom for your honor student

I LOVE CONNIE

My horse bucked off your honor roll student!

Somewhere in Texas, There's a Village Missing an Idiot

Ain't Nothing Meaner than a Marine, 'Cept his Mamma

If You Think My Truck is Smokin',
You Should See My Wife

Fishing stories told here. Some true.

Spay and Neuter Animal
Abusers

Angry. Need a Weapon. Pray Rosary.

I'm not tailgating, I'm drafting

I Like it Dirty
I Like 'em Dropped
Let's Do It

I was normal...
then I bought my first horse.

Behind every good horse
is a human...cleaning up!

If you're gonna ride my bumper
you'd better put a saddle on it!

The Pulse of San Quentin

> *The San Quentin News already circulates inside and outside the prison walls. Its aim is to continue to explore the many ways in which the CDCR is offering extensive programming in educational, vocational, self-help and pre and post release and re-entry classes and counseling.*
>
> —*www.cdcr.ca.gov/Visitors/San_Quentin_News/SQ_newsletter.html*

Do you have a chance of ever getting out of here?

Son, how old are you?

Thirty-five, I reply, looking right back into your eyes.
You shift and lean in closer, answer,
I've been in here since you were five years old. I'm never getting out.

Okay, I reply—awkward, cold,
uncertain.

What I should have said is
I'm sorry. I realize now
this is home for you—you
who have been fundamental
in resurrecting the *San Quentin News*
after sixteen years,
been instrumental in changing attitudes
inside and outside the prison walls,
been the writer who has found
the pen a mighty fortress.

Buckfever

Deer Runs Through Restaurant

SILVER SPRINGS, MD (AP) –*Montgomery County police say a deer being chased by two dogs crashed through a front window of a restaurant before it was put down in the bakery section of a grocery store.*

It's what you call Buckfever,
Maurice over in the bakery says.
Sheriff standin' with his pecker in his hand,
.45 in the other.
Didn't know to shoot or go blind.
Donuts flying, éclairs airborne, smashing all the fresh sourdough.

Ronette, from over in the deli,
come 'round the corner
to see what all the fuss was 'bout,
scolding him right there,
he better put that pistol away, *Right now or help me, Vincent—*
I mean, Sheriff—
you will pay.

Children runnin' around screamin'—
snot pourin' out their noses—goin' blind
from all the fussin' and flying frosting and sprinkles.
Don't think she even seen that deer, just a,
So help me gawd n' I ain't kiddin',
this is my bakery for cries sake!

Ronette, he says, *I need you to remain calm*
and not move a hair.
He drew down on that sonofabitchin' buck—
dropped it like a sack a' feed.

Full Moon Fever

It's 1989, and Tom Petty has packed the Hilton Coliseum in Ames, Iowa.
We've driven too long to see a man on a stage

too far away to reach, but that doesn't matter.
Mom's back in Omaha.

In the middle of the second song of the set—
his new hit *Free Fallin'*—

he stops the song on a dime and addresses all the good people of the world
still filing in from the parking lot.
For all you arriving late, my name's Tom,
and these are the Heartbreakers.

And he hammers that D chord on his Rickenbacker
into a chorus of fire I've never experienced.
Two guys in front of us pass a joint and the temptation
doesn't move us—not this night.

At least they offered,
you say.
We are two men in some nose-bleed section of a palace
of hits in perfect tune with our lives.
Tom takes his usual break, and before the lights come up for Act 2,
a trunk opens behind his mike,
A laser beam of light shoots up
and transforms the stage into a spectacle of wonder
and Tom walks out, reaches in and pulls out
his signature hat.
Too soon the encores end and we mosey
out to the parking lot—speechless,

in a mist of smoke and vibes.
I will go to that night again and again, a fever and aching

that none of us ever let go. We follow a full-moon
on I-80 until we can't drive anymore, and we park

in the lot of some 24-hour diner.
I can't remember if we ate. I can't remember what dream

I was running down then.
I do remember

asking you to pull over, take a break,
telling you I could drive.

There was no need to rush home.
Not sure what was happening

or what true love was.
But it was a haze I didn't mind

being smothered in.

Will You Sell That Eyesore?

Every summer I lived with my grandparents
on Leisure Lake, outside of Trenton, Missouri,
in a house we called a cabin,
built with the help of squirrels like me.

Though I was old enough to know better
than to use the leftover gallon-and-a-half of tan house paint
to customize his beat-up Chevy pickup,
my grandfather, who was spray-painting the truck's paneling with
high-gloss brown he had left over from the gutters—
insisted that I utilize the same brush I'd used on the garage
to paint the cab, doors, and rust.
This truck has got a lot of life left in her yet.

When men have their hands on cans of spray paint
they go to a different world, a place where everyone's an artist.
A little bit more here, and here—
shine her up like new.

For most of an afternoon, we painted and then watched
the truck dry. *Lookee here; pretty as a plate.*
Can't even see the streaks, he said.
Ma will be tickled. Matches the house and everything.

Pretty as a Grit

It's becoming quite ordinary and acceptable
for drivers to stop at lights or stop signs
and immediately stare at their crotches.
Acceptable, as say,
driving my car into a flying cigarette butt.

It has always been hard for me to brake in time,
swerve to miss those glowing embers
all fire-engine red, hot and pink—
that mulatto body soaring to freedom.

It's quite patriotic, really.
All that aggression
sucked to the butt end and then flicked
from your window into my car's grille.
But back to crotches.
I've ruled out hot coffee wedged between legs.
All summer, this blistering heat
makes that assumption ridiculous.
I have not ruled out masturbation,
but that's another story.

When I do honk at you offenders,
I get that "why bother" stare
from my wife, or the finger
from you. So I'm beginning to wonder
what the big deal really is.
Maybe I should just ignore it.
Really, I guess it's kinda pointless.
Like honking at someone after they already
cut you off without warning.
We all know about cigarettes and dumb asses.
They've been known to kill you.

Ink

Fifteen out of twenty-two guys in the class are inked. Blue black brands—their inimitable statements. One of my student's forearms is a mess of calligraphy, and when I lean down to read his arm horizontally it says LIFE—when he turns his arm upside down, DEATH. Interesting, I say out loud, and it is. Someone put a lot of thought into that. I ask the other students in class to write down their tattoos on a piece of paper, or show me if they prefer. One asks, *Do you have a tattoo, Dr. Reese?* And I put my leg up on the desk and pull up my pant leg, push down my black sock. *GONZO.*

What does that say? Gonzo?

What's that supposed to mean?

It means immersing yourself in the story—instead of writing about someone getting a tattoo, you go get one yourself and tell everyone how it feels to be permanently marked.

Outside this prison, body art is a statement—a mark of authority.

M.O.B. Money Over Bitches

Loose Lips Sink Ships

What Is, Will Be

Loyalty: Born 2 Fail, Destined 2 Succeed, Death B4 Dishonor. Soldier

Virgin Mary Jesus Christ Heart Rose

Wild Wild 100's

Suckafree

And on the eyelids of one man there are two tattoos that read—*GAME OVER.*

In here, as I watch men peel off layers of themselves—stripped of freedom, some trying to find redemption, I still question them. *Who the hell has the tattoo—Fuck the ATF DEA US Marshals—?*

And I see X put down his head, his face turns red. He slowly raises his hand, kinda grins.

I seen it, another classmate of his says. *It's on his back.* And immediately I flash back to high school, in some cramped apartment drinking a forty with god knows who, some Nazi punk with SKINS tattooed across his forehead backwards. I tell the class the story. How we all hated the kid but didn't know what to do. They laugh. Cuss under their breath. Shake their heads. X is deadpan, looking out the iron window.

The Relaxer

In Chicago O'Hare, I stop at
the back rub place,
pay my twenty dollars for
the "Relaxer."

I'm peering over the privacy partition trying
to see which woman I would like to rub me down,
trying desperately to avoid the man to my left
cracking his knuckles.

You have back problem? The man asks.
No, I tell him. And I'm back up on my toes
gawking at the pretty women rubbing their hands
through hair—their soft, delicate touch.
Come. Lajos will fix your back. He says.
I've already paid the twenty bucks,
so I do what I'm told.

If it hurts too much, tell Lajos.
Lajos will fix back problem.
My face is buried in a paper towel;
my body slumped in a portable massage chair.
He starts in, elbowing me in the back
and grinding on my spine.

You carry stress here, he says.
And here.

He starts deep rubbing the sides of my
lower back and then does some number
on my arms—trying to shake out my enormous
biceps.
Hey, Lajos, I say through the paper towel.
That's where I release my stress.
He chuckles.
Chicken wing, he says.

I paid good money
for this private intrusion—a foreigner
rubbing, tearing at my limbs.
All I hear is the security level is yellow,
elevated, significant risk—remain cautious,
and some funky relaxation music, and Lajos saying,
Here, much pain. Lajos fix.
And to be honest, I don't want him
to stop.

He rubs my scalp, stretches my arms in directions
they've never gone before, claps his hands—*done.*
Like newborn, yes?
You bet. I tell him.
And I'm off,
all bright-eyed,
for new destinations.

Breast Man

It always seems to occur
over the carving of the turkey.
That awkward holiday moment,
the man and his knife, too many beers
too soon in the afternoon.
Say, you a breast man, ain't you?

I've never asked anyone
if they're a breast man.
White or dark, sure. I'll eat
either meat. Especially the thighs.

But back to breasts—celebrating them.
I do wish to pay tribute
like so many of my fellows,
but to be honest with you,
I'm not a breast man,
and I'll tell you why.

More than a handful, Denise Hillside was
in eighth grade. The couples' skate was
odd. Denise, at least a foot taller than me—
foot-and-a-half with her roller skates on.
Knockers (that's what Charlie Ferguson called them)
the size of my shoulders and biceps.

It's one thing to look up to the woman you adore,
but to maneuver through those obstacles,
my face suffocating in her chest—
all that intimidation;
you understand?
After losing myself a few too many times,
I looked for a companion more my size.

A woman friend of mine, who is not a breast person,
insisted one night that we go to a strip club—now!
We're practically there already, she slurred,
sitting on a downtown bench. And
who was I or the other couple
to disagree?

After watching a few pole dances, she exclaimed,
All these women have fake boobs—
none of those are real!
And another woman in the audience smiled;
they seemed to have a mutual understanding,
a sisterhood not of traveling pants—but of boobs.

We all finished our drinks and walked away
feeling larger, and strangely more buoyant,
than we did when we arrived.

Scratch and Win

7:45 at night, the girls dumping bath water
on each other, the floor, the phone rings.
Are you getting the girls to bed?
My mother-in-law asks.

Yes, and I'm picking up this Christmas tree
that just fell over.

I bet you maybe had some help with that.
Say, did you get that car key in the mail? The mailer says
if your winning number matches the number
in the mailer, then you could win one of four prizes;
a new car or truck, even. I don't need a truck, but I
could use that car. And my numbers match.
Did you scratch your number off?

No. It's in the recycle.

Okay then, I'll let you go. I just wondered if I should drive up
and see if I'm really a winner.

No, no. Wait a second. I'll go check.

I rummage through old magazines and paper
and find the key to my new car—I scratch off
a gray circle and pick up the phone:

Here's my winning number: 931418.

Oh, hell, it's a scam, she says.
We both can't be winners.

And so it goes. The artificial tree will survive
the night. I toss the key back into the recycle and
return to the winners in the tub.

Yard Work

Forgive, O Lord, my little jokes on thee, and I'll forgive thy great big joke on me.

—Robert Frost

Word on the yard is
you don't like poems that rhyme.
Ain't that what poetry's all about?

Please tell the yard I have been misquoted.
What most concerns me is rhythm,
not rhyme.

Just tellin' you what people're sayin'.
Ever since I can remember,
poetry rhymed.

Fifty Shades of Grey

The woman next to me on a treadmill
is reading her new Kindle and the text has been
enlarged. I look over to try and figure out what has her
so engrossed. I read,

"Does this mean you're going to make love to me tonight, Christian?"

Holy shit. Did I just read that?

His mouth drops open slightly, but he recovers quickly.
"No, Anastasia it doesn't. Firstly, I don't make love. I....

I lose my footing. Damn. That's a good part.

...and thirdly, you don't yet know what you're in for. You could still run for the hills. Come, I want to show you my playroom."

She sees me glancing at her tablet. She turns a bit red
in the face.

Good book? I ask.

Oh, yes. A friend of mine just bought me this.
Easy on the eyes.

I bet.

She continues her cardiovascular workout,
moving a bit faster now.

Don't tell anyone but I downloaded Fifty Shades of Grey.
The first of a trilogy.
I've been going at it for three weeks, now.
I'm a slow reader.

Sunshine, Handcuffs, Plexiglass, Scars

See these flowers, a student says. *They're closed at night and in the morning they open—stay open most of the day. I don't know what they're called, but I get to see them open and close every day. I had these same flowers by my front steps. The stems feel plastic, almost fake. They break easily. We aren't supposed to touch them here.*

You know, one of the prisons they had me at, I could step into a corner of my cell and get a sliver of sunlight—it would hit me right here. He cranes his neck and closes his eyes. *Right here on my face for about a half an hour. That was the only sunlight I'd see. It's mental deprivation. It works.*

Hell, most guards don't know what you're in for. They don't care. We were loaded on a 747 one winter and we were standing on the tarmac without any jackets—bunch of us. Just a t-shirt and orange pants, no socks, no shoes. They had our legs chained at the ankles so tight I was bleeding all over my feet—freezing. Scars are still here. He puts his leg onto a bench and pulls down his sock to show me.

You know, I'm no killer or sicko. My whole stint that got me here lasted only five months. That's how long it took me to hit bottom. Hanging out with some terrible people I thought were my friends and I backslid down the whole way that fast. Meth will eat you up. Fifteen years I'll be down for an addiction I couldn't shake—could have never imagined.

When my daughter used to come visit me, I'd be behind those glass partitions—she'd tell me Daddy, roll down this window. I'd say I can't honey. She'd ask when are you gonna come home? Soon, I'd tell her. Now she wants to know the date. She'll be graduated by then.

Unlimited Absolutes

Get your ass up off the couch
and get a job! We're broke and
I'm pregnant. A student standing outside my office
screams into her cell phone. *There. You know, now.*

All these broke students with their unlimited plans,
unlimited minutes to text and converse—how I love
your absolutes. No money for infant formula.
No money for lunch;
but there you are hunched over,
fingers moving frantically,
showing the world the top of your head.
I often imagine your lifelines
gone sour—no bars to connect. You're stranded
on the shoulder of Highway 81 unable to drive—
pounding your head
against the window.
Now what!

I might stop to help. But not today.
Today I'm grading stories about runners.
Everyone is running this semester,
cataloging the city and explaining in great detail
the taint in their pants.
Runners find this humorous—
a casual conversational piece.

One essay warns us about too much coffee
before a morning run.
One finds it necessary to go into great detail
about remnants left on the soles of his shoes.
I lay dying here in your defecations—these woes
that mold you.

I wanted to be loved once.
And at the end of the story isn't that what we all ask for?

Potatoes in the Dryer

Guess where I put my potatoes, the anonymous woman says,
dropping off a box of FFA potatoes at our house.

Twenty six dollars for about ninety russets—
are in my dryer. It's 50 degrees in there.

In my mind I see her burrowing through a junk drawer
to find a thermometer that still works. This
in the home of a family deeply concerned
with how hot or cold a room should be—
how to appropriately insulate and save—
how to overheat and suffocate.

I imagine the anonymous woman placing the thermometer
in the dryer—waiting, re-checking again and again until
she's certain this is just as good as digging a big hole out back
or placing them in the cellar she no longer has.
You trying to invent some kinda slow-cooker,
or a new way to make mashed potatoes?

Once more the anonymous woman looks at me strangely
but doesn't tell mc how hopelessly incompetent she thinks I am.

The Doctor vs. the Pre-Med Student

Finals week and in a college bathroom
I find a note that reads:

Perform frequent neurological checks on the client.

I think of the student whose nervous system is already shot—
who is hiding answers to questions
in toilet paper dispensers.

I think of this clever student as almost
getting accepted to med school.
I think of this pre-med student as a neurologist,
which scares me.

Postgraduate and clinical training—
the 10-12 years of tests.
Your own therapeutic spinal tap to relieve
the increased pressure.

I think of this neurologist watching the box-set DVDs of Grey's Anatomy
one too many times. *Don't you remember George?*
He asks his medical colleagues. *How he struggled so?*

I think of your eye-crossing vision—you balancing on one leg.
Who on earth let you pass the sobriety check that mattered?
How often you recite the alphabet backwards in public and
make the others at the bar buy you a drink when they try and fail.

Did you know, in Germany, a compulsory year of psychiatry
must be done to complete a residency of neurology?
I didn't. I get my neurological facts
on Wikipedia.

I'm no doctor—
well, actually I am, but not the kind that can feel you—
but please, start referring to your clients
as patients, start seeing them
as human beings.

Cattle Drive

The trouble with the semis in my town
is that they offend some visitors.
The stench of overcrowded trailers, excrement.
White marquee above their cabs advertising:
Last Ride
CowTaxi
See Ya!
We'll Be OK.

The first time I saw these I laughed my ass off.
It's no wonder when a guest writer and extremely vocal vegan
was visiting I was so eager to point a truck out to her.
That's filth, she said.

No, I told her. *That's dinner.*

Where I'm Going, Where I've Been

Most days in the education building
at this prison camp
you'll find a man tracing one of the large maps
of the United States with his finger.

Sometimes groups huddle around the maps.
One man talking about adventure. Another showing
a childhood birthplace. Another exclaiming, *where I'm gonna go*
once I'm outta here. Find me a job and do it up right.
Gonna be a father this time 'round.

I stand at the map during break.
I trace the Missouri River south. Find its confluence, the
Mississippi. Follow it down and down.

An inmate walks by, says, *Anywhere but here.*
Anywhere but here.

Saluting Lieutenant Jones

Make no mistake. We are experts in the application of violence... Your conscience should be clear. Your honor should be clean.

—from *Hell and Back Again,* a film by Danfung Dennis

Good morning ladies and gentlemen.
On behalf of Delta flight 3144,
I'd like you to help me welcome
our United States soldiers flying with us today.

In line for our security check,
families surround us in camouflage
and tears. Young children clutching onto
fathers and mothers unlacing boots,
departing for duty.

I don't know why we gotta keep sending these kids
over there to the Middle East.
We have to take care of ourselves—this country.
Two guys behind me comment.
Hell, they been fighting wars over there
for thousands' a years.
Ain't anything we can do to change them.

On this forty-four minute flight to Minneapolis,
C-17 Globemaster all enormous and gray,
carrying kids to Afghanistan—
to hell.
US Air Force Lieutenant Jones is in tears.

Occasionally I look between seats to see
if he's okay. Now he's red-faced.
Now he's stone-faced.
I want to reach back to him,
find out his first name. Buy him a drink.
Get him bombed out of his mind so he can forget
at least for this short amount of time.

Hell, Jones, I'm sorry no one is talking.
And these are just black words on white paper.
We're all scared to know
what's happening here,
what's maybe ending
now.

Still and Silent as Stone

After dinner-count, I see you
on the stairwell gazing
out the large turn-of-century windows,
each pane a looking glass
into that world where you once belonged.

I never say hello to you.
You don't see me looking down these stairs at your back,
your khaki shirt, your gray, receding hair.

I climb the next flight,
look out the window to see
if I can decipher what it is you are fixed on—parking lot?
Midday traffic? Over the fence are homes.
Families racing about.
A kid on a skateboard ollies over a manhole.
Two speed-walkers point and chatter as they chase each other.

But shit, man,
maybe I have it all wrong.
I see the Chevys and Fords, hear the engines call,
the glass-pack's throaty cough.

Maybe we're more alike than I thought,
waiting patiently, considering that getaway car.

The Hard Nutcracker

I slept through "The Nutcracker" in third grade.
Here I am, nearly 40, dancing in the ballet.
So what color tights do you get to wear?
My colleagues ask.

For the past two months I've been catching myself
standing pointe in the kitchen while stirring
the goulash—at any unsuspecting sound,
I turn to check the wall behind me.

My students have begun staring
strangely at me. One says,
Did you sprain your ankle or something?
All the world's a stage, and all the men and women merely players, I tell them.
Metaphor. Shakespeare.
Look him up. And if you must know,
I'm dancing in the ballet with my daughter and wife.
I bow and flutter my wrists to show them
I am not embarrassed.
You can dance! Another student exclaims more than asks.

I want to mention the six-degree separation I have
with Kevin Bacon. Remind them of the first *Footloose.*
How I danced in front of the movie screen up and down the aisle
with my mother because we could as the blockbuster ended and
the credits rolled.
Show them old Run–D.M.C. videos—find my boom-box
and pop a few locks. But instead I tell them,
There are things you will do for love, someday, young
grasshoppers, that will make all the difference.

During these six-hour dress rehearsals
the girls are in the wing, crying.
Girls backstage practicing splits,
girls in the ring, fighting…
Girls on stage, dreaming,
girls bending and pivoting,
relacing satin pointe shoes to appear weightless and
sylph-like, lifting to become one with Marie Taglioni.

All the world's a stage, I whisper to my daughter, before it's her cue.
They haven't kicked us out yet.

Medley

I work in a prison.
My three-and-a-half-year-old daughter, Paige,
knows this. People have told her,
Your daddy works at a prison.
That's where they put mean bad people.

Someday, I will tell her
what it is I do there—that I teach men to write,
to come to terms with their emotional instabilities
that brought them there.

Today, when she asks for more chicken nuggets,
I ask her if she has finished her vegetables.
Well, actually no. I am saving them, she says.

Actually is such a big word, Paige. I'm so proud of you.
But actually, you'll have to eat some vegetables first,
or you will have to go to prison.

I get up from the table,
lower my head and put my hands behind my back.
I pretend to walk in shackles.
They cuff you up, and you'll have to eat your vegetables without
any silverware. I keep pacing around the kitchen
and stop to bob for vegetables from my plate.
I come up for air, a mess of lima beans and peas.

Paige begins to cry.
Her sister, Willow, who is seven-and-a-half, says,
That's not funny, Dad.

Not only have I reinforced their fear of prison.
I have ruined vegetable medley.
Being a father isn't easy.
Being funny isn't either.

New Folsom Prison Blues

There are few words for
razor on flesh—for scream.
Black. Blue. Cut. Wet.

I see some of you bandaged at the wrist,
forearm, belly, throat.
You are cutting to get out.

If we treat men like animals they'll eventually
start to chew their way out—

We know this,
now.

German Dressing and Black Velvet

In Leisure Lanes Trailer Park
we would gather to watch soundless home movies.
Grandpa with his Black Velvet on the rocks;
you, Grandmother with Scotch tape, hitting the lights on and off
to fix the reel whenever the film split in two.
Even then you were always mending, fixing.

One night I remember the film clicking, the picture
shaky as always on the white pop-up screen in the middle of
the living room. There you were dancing, smiling,
playing on a beach I'd never been to. You were wearing a
corset swimming suit.
I remember how I put my foot in my mouth
when I said, *Look, Grandma's pregnant.*

Mother turned and glared at me, but I didn't know what
I had just said. *But mom,* I said again, *You're there
and all your sisters—where's the other baby
Grandma had?*

There was never another baby—just childhood honesty,
questions I didn't know the answers to yet. Things like
how a woman works her whole life to support a man and her children
and how a child's curiosity can bring a grown woman to tears.

Grandma, I apologize now like
I did then. All summer I have been digging in photo boxes
and today I took your funeral eulogy off the corkboard
in the kitchen. One of the last things you ever told me –
We always thought of you as the son we never had.

One of the last nights at your home, Grandpa
told us you were forgetting to make dinner,
forgetting to eat at all. His shaky voice praying for someone
to help him as you had done all those years.

Maybe you did forget some things that didn't
seem important in the end. But I haven't forgotten.
I keep your dressing recipe taped
to the cupboard:

Sugar (to taste)
Miracle Whip 3-4 TBSP
Milk (to taste)
Celery Seed
White Vinegar (optional)
Mix and serve cold

Kindly ask for an extra plate.
Leave skin on and slop the potato with real butter.
Heap on the lettuce, drench plate with dressing.
Look at your flank steak, consider it with eggs in the morning.
Devour potatoes and silage one after the other.

The Woman Who Wishes to Remain Anonymous Goes Shopping for a Power Sheep

My father-in-law drives the woman who wishes to remain anonymous
to my house. He will sit in his favorite rocking-chair he has given us
and watch our 46-inch high definition television.
The woman with him wants me to take her shopping.
She has been comparing prices,
like she always does,
for more than a month. She wants me to help her
pick out the right weed-whacker.
Those knees of his have been bothering him something terrible.
I've been doing all the mowing.

She thinks I know a little more than the next guy
when it comes to purchasing these things.
I appreciate that. And I am not taking this task lightly.
To be honest, I already have one picked out.
A 29cc 4-Cycle Straight Shaft Trimmer.
She won't go for it—it's the top of the line
and more power than she needs.
But,
I have to at least try.

We visit the first store. She has trouble lifting
the one I have chosen, so I don't push the issue.
The eager salesman is bombarded with questions
for nearly twenty minutes until he excuses himself
to use the restroom.

We visit the second store. A mega-mart
and no one is around to help.

We visit the third store with over fourteen
weed-whackers to choose from.
We compare lithium batteries to plug-in
trimmers, extended warranties to prices,
prices back to warranties, plug-ins back to
battery life.

Well, she says,
studying the Yard Man and its curved shaft trimmer—no
oil and gas mixing, EZ Start for comfort and convenience—
I like this one.
Good warranty. Should last me
'til I'm dead.

Gothic Chic

There's always a sun
in my daughters' drawings—big and yellow
with sharp rays extending from its
core. Two or more bizarre people are always holding hands,
and more than likely there's an awkward-looking
heart in the picture. An upside-down triangle split where
two halves make a whole.
Thank god for that. What if they only painted
gray haze and smoke stacks—black cats?
What if all they wanted to do was use their periwinkle
for lipstick and then devour the crayon?

Prison Thermos

Really, I'd never given much thought
to it. A thermos.
But here, they are trademarks.
Your identity. Walking with instant
freeze-dried coffee, milk on ice, Tang.
Decals stuck to your insulated canisters.
Some of them family trees and longing eyes.
A picture of your child in second grade—
bright-eyed, big glasses and missing front teeth.
Some, cut-outs from magazines. An ass. A G-string.
Leather breasts on the back of a Harley. 6x6 antlers.
Trophies toasting these ounces of freedom
they haven't yet stripped away.

Wishing Well

Each one of us makes a myth of the soul we imagine ours.
So mythic we'll never vanish.

—Kevin Clark

This morning in the hallway
I find a note on the floor:
I hope my mom and DaD don't Diy forevre.

My daughter does this sometimes, leaves notes.
She tries to ignore me as I hold the letter
in my hand and ask, *What's this*?
She turns her back and acts disgusted.
I don't push the issue.
But, all day I approach the note in my head
from different angles.
Is she scared? Has she been watching too much TV?
How do I tell a six-year-old
that we will all die someday?

Later, after exhausting myself
with the right thing to say, I think
soon enough she'll want me dead—not seriously
gone for good, just out of the picture.
When she's a teenager, all that freedom she'll be aching for,
like the other day she screams at me,
Dad! I can get out of the car by myself. Thanks for the ride.
And she's out of the car running down the small hill into school,
her enormous pink backpack smacking the backs
of her calves.

A friend of mine told me,
You can't be friends with your kids.
And I know what he means; we can't just be friends.
That'll come down the road, when they are gone
to train orcas, and wrestle with the other
predators of the sea.

I also know I'll never stop
being their father. As I get older,
I'll still need them to ask me for advice.
Like, *What the hell is a basin wrench for*? Or,
Why do you care about that so much?
I realize our relationship will continue
to evolve, like mine with my father and mother,
how we occasionally butt heads.
Now parenthood is becoming a bit more clear.

Down

i've been down.

Been down since '91.

i've been down goin' on nine years, now.

Been down at three prisons. This here's

the cream of the crop.

i count my time in Ajax bottles.

You know how many cinder blocks are in my room? 236.

Hell, this is a caste system they trying to run in this country.

Down

Down

Fear Down

Dread walking this flat yard forever.

Ask me how many of us are nonviolent offenders; just ask me.

You know how much money i cost taxpayers since i been down?

i don't know if i can survive. if i leave here, what will I do? what can i legitimately do to make some money—all these bills waiting for me when i get out.

Ain't nothing left for me out there. Lost it all.

Hell, i'm just a short timer.

That's how i caught my case. Lying to myself every day. Gets easy. Day in day out. it's just a lie.

Man, you don't understand what it's like to be down. You weren't born a criminal.

Man, what you talking about? You weren't born a criminal, neither.

The Actuary

I suppose it was the ritual
that caught my attention first.
My father's ties neatly aligned.
The suits color-coordinated,
pressed and hanging in his closet.

Before morning rush hour,
this man appeared in the kitchen
spinning the gold combination code of his briefcase—
that familiar pop of air and the business inside.
Then the double-checking of its contents
and the vacuum-sealed closure
of an actuary.

Every time I asked what he did,
he'd roll his eyes
and look at me deadpan. *It's complicated. You wouldn't understand.*
You see, he never brought work home with him.
It stayed bottled inside that briefcase.

My mother on the other hand,
who always worked late, uncorked
her day's dilemmas at dinner with a red zin or noir.
I'd remember her co-workers' names, often pretending
that my goulash was the insides of their brains.
Look mom, I'm eating that dick Jerry's brain.

How cool and collected one side of the table seemed,
while those of us on the other side were
dripping daggers and gulping blood.

On the days I pressed my father,
he'd say things like *risk*—that he analyzed
future financial events.
Predictions. Mortality. Insurance. Loss.
Part fortune-teller. Part advisor. But all math.

You never heard my father say actuaries were super-heroes.
The headhunters who called for him on a regular basis,
when he refused to answer the phone anymore,
asked me time and time again
to leave those messages for him.

Work is the ritual that drives my family still.
Even me, the college professor
with my sports jacket and tie—
razor-burned neck.
My daughters now leave me Post-it notes in the closet:
Dad, wear this ty today. I hope it matchs.
I'm a teacher. I advise. I predict.
I analyze and hypothesize.

There's a crystal ball on my desk.
Oh, baloney. On my desk is a flying pig.
I can't predict anyone's outcome, but
I'm learning to believe in all this paraphernalia.
When I stare at that boar long enough,
I'm reminded how far anyone can come.

The Blues in Jeans

When I found the sewing needle
in the crotch of my newly hemmed jeans,
I was troubled.
Not for the nut sack that had gone
unharmed, but for my overall well-being.
My mother-in-law had done the sewing—
perhaps forgetful, perhaps not.
An instinctive shriveling
in the un-hemmed crotch
rendered my jeans somewhat roomier
than I remembered.

April's Proposal

It's April Fool's Day in South Dakota.
Our eight-year-old daughter has just killed
the first fly of the season with a velvet-lined
jewelry box. *No time for a fly swatter,* she says,
so I used this. She holds the box up in the air
proposing I do something with it.
Paige, her younger sister, asks to see
the fly for the second time.
Oooouuuuu, she says. *You got that good, Willow.*

I only hope when someone
is proposing to either of them
that they think of this unseasonably warm day on the Great Plains,
almost 92 degrees, and say *Oooooouuuu*
after squashing it.

Thunder-n-Lightning

It's tourney time, and my daughter, Willow,
has just scored her second run this season—
the innings Mercy Rule follows.
Team Thunder hits the field as I strap the catcher's gear onto
one of the unlucky players. She's already drenched.
It's ninety degrees, muggy as all get-out—
a storm brewing.

My wife is in the stands, making faces at me, which is always
a good sign, and our other daughter, Paige, is chasing
ground squirrels with the other kids too young to play.
I'm helping coach and keep score with two other fathers
as the girls open up their first can of whoop-ass
against the opposing team.

We fetchin' or catchin' here, girls?—the eight-year-old
third baseman hollers.
And 1,2,3 we are back to the top of our line-up
and the chatter begins.
Can you turn around like Michael Jackson?
Break down like Britney Spears?
Shake it off like Salt-n-Pepa?
No You Can't!

With cheeks full of sunflower seeds,
these girls are starting to gel.
How beautiful it is to see them come together as a team,
discovering the beauty of the game before it's ruined
by adults.

Tonight after ice cream, I water the red maple,
the first tree we've ever planted. The girls run
and chase fireflies.
When they catch one, they can't help but
hold it hostage and pull its wings.
I just can't stand to see it suffer, Willow says.

She grabs the hose
and begins drowning the thing.

Soon enough they are off for a new adventure.
As I watch my new As-Seen-on-TV Pocket Hose
ravel itself into a ball, I catch a glimpse of what's left
of the firefly—its cold light smeared on cement,
and I hear on this particularly quiet night,
the flurry of small wings ascending.

General Equivalency Diploma

Hey, I passed—I really did it!

Two inmate students high-five each other.

Way to go man! I told you
you could do it.
The one pats the other on the back.

White men Red men Yellow men Black men
all happy to be graduating. Their smiles frozen on Polaroid—
ear to ear to sky, soaring alone now—
free.

GED test result day is always fun
around here, the Education Director says.

Really Happy

And, like me, he misses the old days, when talking to yourself meant you were crazy, back when being crazy was a big deal, not just an acronym or something you could take a pill for. I liked it when people who were talking to themselves might actually have been talking to God or an angel. You respected people like that.
—George Bilgere

Take highway 81 north, just over the Missouri River bridge, and merge onto Broadway—this is river city—dirt's grime and chime. There he is with the worn jacket, sun-faded red, white and blue hoodie.

Listen. He's belting his guts out again, all the way up these four lanes. Broadway is humming with cattle trucks on their way to the world's largest livestock auction, jake brakes and texters—all of these pilgrims haulin' ass north to a colder Dakota or scoopin' the loop out of boredom. You can hear him above the din. Some days he's pedaling and now he's be-boppin' on foot, singing what sounds to be Dylan's *Tambourine Man* or is that Sly's *THANK YOU FALETTINME BE MICE ELF AGIN?*

The other day my daughter asks—*Is he wacko?*
He's having a good time is what I tell her.

And today, because of our own cabin fever, we are packed in the car looking for him—windows down, a cold January wind filling the cab. There he is turning onto 25th, then Fox Run Parkway on his way to the global super-center for a new pair of socks; or maybe to some human behavior center where they'll ask him to take off his headphones and talk with the others. We cheer him on; let him take his time at the crosswalk, his right hand waving and left hand clutching the radio. He doesn't miss a beat, banging that imaginary snare and floor tom.

That's the guy who saved rock and roll, my daughter says.
Yes, indeed, I respond.

And I feel happier than I have in days—my daughters in the back, all smiles, bobbing their heads up and down to their own music.

He keeps right on going past the South Dakota tradition, a 12,000 square foot machine shed where this weekend it's all you can handle crab legs and mountain oysters. He's not after food. He's not stopping at any gas station casino for his cash crop. Doesn't stop at the floral shop—nor does he need a tune-up. He pays no attention to the three whiz kids on the other side of the road playing swords—pissing into the wind. Doesn't seem to give a rip about much of anything except the rhythm of the guitar, that thump thump thumping of the bass and his own irreducible voice.

Jim Reese is an Associate Professor of English; Director of the Great Plains Writers' Tour at Mount Marty College in Yankton, South Dakota; and Editor-in-Chief of *PADDLEFISH.* Reese's poetry and prose have been widely published, most recently in *New York Quarterly, Poetry East, Paterson Literary Review, Louisiana Literature Review, Connecticut Review,* and elsewhere. His book *ghost on 3rd* was a Finalist for the 2010 Milt Kessler Poetry Award. Other recent awards include a 2012 Allen Ginsberg Poetry Award and a 2012 Distinguished Public Service Award in recognition of Reese's exemplary dedication and contributions to the Education Department at the Yankton Federal Prison Camp. Since 2008, Reese has been one of six artists-in-residence throughout the country who are part of the National Endowment for the Art's interagency initiative with the Department of Justice's Federal Bureau of Prisons.

photo by Jamie Ridgway

Reese and his family live in southern South Dakota, near John Wesley Powell's one hundredth meridian—better than most determinants for where the American West begins.

CPSIA information can be obtained
at www.ICGtesting.com
Printed in the USA
FSOW04n1826210316
18233FS